A Pocket Guide to

The Mass

A Pocket Guide to
The Mass

Michael Dubruiel

Our Sunday Visitor Publishing Division
Our Sunday Visitor, Inc.
Huntington, Indiana 46750

"Truly, truly, I say to you, unless you eat the flesh of the Son of man and drink his blood, you have no life in you."
— JOHN 6:53

Contents

Introduction

In a book written before his election as Pope Benedict XVI, then Cardinal Joseph Ratzinger wrote of the dangers of the Mass losing its moorings — as the worship of God. He compared the present situation to that of the people of Israel, who in the desert, waiting for Moses to come down from the mountain, found God to be distant and aloof, leading them to conceive a ritual that was a celebration of the community alone. He wrote in *The Spirit of the Liturgy*, "Instead of being worship of God, it becomes a circle closed in on itself: eating, drinking, and making merry."[1] This type of worship, he says, offers "no experience of that liberation which always takes place when man encounters the living God."[2]

This little book is meant to help you to experience that liberation — that freedom — from distress that comes when we forget that there is a God and that our very existence has everything to do with worshipping Him.

The way that God has chosen to bring about this encounter with humanity is through His Son Jesus Christ. It is Christ who has revealed God to us and instituted the celebration of the Eucharist as a means of perpetually bringing about this encounter between God and man — until Our Lord returns in glory.

In this book you will find the following:

- Answers to basic questions about the Mass
- Definitions of the lesser-known words used in the Mass
- The biblical origins of many of the prayers used in the Mass
- How to use the experience of the two disciples on the road to Emmaus (Luke 24:13–35) as a way to understand the Mass

This book is meant to be a simple guide. For a more in-depth look at the Mass, you might want to read my easy-to-understand books *The How-To Book of the Mass* and *How to Get the Most Out of the Eucharist.* For an excellent missal that will give you the Church's prayers, responses, and readings as they vary throughout the year, I highly recommend the beautiful *Daily Roman Missal.* All of these publications are available from Our Sunday Visitor publishing.

What Is the Mass?

The Names of the Mass

Catholics call the celebration of the Lord's Supper a variety of names:

- The Eucharist *(a Greek term meaning "thanksgiving")*
- The Liturgy *(a word that means "work," literally the work of the Lord)*
- The Holy Sacrifice *(after both the sacrifice of Christ and that of the Faithful)*
- The Offering *(referring to Jesus' offering to the Father and to His disciples)*
- The Breaking of the Bread *(referring to what Jesus did at the Last Supper)*
- The Lord's Supper *(referring to Jesus' institution of the Mass)*
- The Wedding Banquet of the Lord *(reflecting the Book of Revelation's term for the Mass)*

But it is likely that you know it as the Mass.

Why do we call it the Mass?

Mass is an English rendering of the Latin term "*missa*." In Latin, the Mass ends with the words "*Ite, missa est*," which translated into English means, "Go forth, you are sent." We get the word "dismissal" and "missal" from the Latin word "*missa*." So, even though we gather for the celebration of the Mass, its name implies that we are focused on being sent on a mission by Our Lord.

What are the parts of the Mass?

Traditionally, the Mass had been divided into two parts: The Mass of the Catechumens and The Mass of the Faithful. The "catechumens" were those who were not fully members of the Church and were "dismissed" at the end of the Mass of the Catechumens (after the homily). Today this part of the Mass is referred to as the Liturgy of the Word. The "faithful" are those who have been baptized and would remain until they were sent forth at the end of the second part of the Mass, now referred to as the Liturgy of the Eucharist.

Where does the Mass come from?

Jesus Christ, on the night before he died, celebrated the Jewish Passover meal with his disciples at the Last Supper. In the course of the meal, He gave new meaning to the ritual, declaring the bread that He blessed, broke, and gave to His disciples to be His Body, and the cup filled with wine to be His Blood that was of the New Covenant. Where Moses had taken the blood of a sacrificed bull to ratify the Covenant of Sinai (see Exodus 24:3–8), Jesus offered Himself by his Passion and Death and offered His Body and Blood under the forms of bread and wine to His disciples to seal the New Covenant. His instruction to His apostles to do it "in remembrance of me" (1 Corinthians 11:25) continues to be fulfilled every time we gather for Mass.

Where do the prayers of the Mass come from?

The prayers used at Mass have developed over the Church's history. Many of them are taken directly from the Bible, and one prayer, the

Creed, comes from several early Church councils (worldwide gatherings of bishops to discuss Church matters). Throughout this small book, we will look at the Biblical origins of many of the common prayers used at Mass. At every Mass, there are many times when the people gathered and the priest are literally quoting Scripture to each other in their communal worship of God.

Where do the readings we hear at the Mass come from?

The readings we hear proclaimed at the Mass are all from the Bible. The First Reading is either from the Old Testament or the Acts of the Apostles (during the Easter Season). The Responsorial Psalm is from the Book of Psalms. The Second Reading is from one of the New Testament Letters or the Book of Revelation. The Gospel Reading is always from one of the four Gospels.

How is the Mass a sacrifice?

The Mass makes present the one sacrifice of Jesus on the cross at Calvary. All who participate in the Mass join their spiritual sacrifices to the one sacrifice of Christ, and through Him, they are offered to God the Father through the action of the Holy Spirit.

What is the sacrifice I offer at Mass?

Yourself — at Baptism we died to ourselves so that we might live in Christ. At the Mass, the Body of Christ gathers as one, acting not individually but as Christ. So at Mass our movements (standing, sitting, kneeling, and so on) are governed by the Church. Our speech is not of our own choosing, but rather we speak the Word of God. We sacrifice our own choices to be one in Christ. We offer the sacrifice of our weaknesses to receive instruction from the Word of the Lord and nourishment from the Body and Blood of Christ so that we can be transformed into Christ.

Why is the Mass called the "source and summit of the Christian Life"?[3]

Through our participation, and by offering our sacrifice at Mass, we are formed by God's Word and brought into Communion with Him through our reception of the Blessed Sacrament. The Mass is our opportunity to learn from Christ, to die to ourselves in order to live in Him, and, by listening to Him, to be given sight to recognize Him in the many guises in which He comes to us in our daily lives (see Matthew 25).

A Prayer to Say before Mass

Almighty and ever-living God, I approach the sacrament of your only-begotten Son, our Lord Jesus Christ. I come sick to the doctor of life, unclean to the fountain of mercy, blind to the radiance of eternal light, and poor and needy to the Lord of heaven and earth.

Lord, in your great generosity, heal my sickness, wash away my defilement, enlighten my blindness, enrich my poverty, and clothe my nakedness. May I receive the bread of angels, the King of kings and Lord of lords, with humble reverence, with the purity and faith, the repentance and love, and the determined purpose that will help to bring me to salvation. May I receive the Sacrament of the Lord's Body and Blood and its reality and power.

Kind God, may I receive the Body of your only-begotten Son, our Lord Jesus Christ, born from the womb of the Virgin Mary, and so be received into His mystical Body and numbered among his members.

Loving Father, as on my earthly pilgrimage I now receive your beloved Son under the veil of a sacrament, may I one day see Him face to face in glory, who lives and reigns with you forever.

Amen.

— St. Thomas Aquinas

The Parts of the Mass

On the following pages you will find useful information about the various parts of the Mass, including the following:

Speaking the Bible — Because many of the prayers that we say at every Mass are taken from the Bible, we are "speaking" the Bible when we say these prayers. Here we will show you where the prayer occurs in the Bible and its context. The words that we say at Mass are in bold within these texts.

What does it mean? — Some of the words we say at Mass are not translated from the original Hebrew or Greek. Here we define, in English, what they mean.

What is it? — Some of the names of sacred vessels used at Mass may be foreign to you. Here we describe what they are.

Posture, Gesture, or Silence — Often the most confusing aspect of the Mass for the uninitiated, and sometimes even the lifelong Catholic, is what they should be doing with their body at times throughout the Mass and during the times of silence. Here, we describe the "how" and the "why."

INTRODUCTORY RITES

Entering the Church Building

- When you enter a Catholic Church for the celebration of Mass, you first bless yourself with Holy Water from either a font (small bowl) near the door or the Baptismal font located near the entrance of the Church.
- Before entering your pew or seat, you genuflect toward the Blessed Sacrament in the tabernacle (look for a lit sanctuary lamp) or, if the reservation of the Blessed Sacrament is in a side chapel, bow toward the altar.
- Then, kneeling or sitting, you spend some time recollecting yourself in prayer (you could pray "A Prayer to Say before Mass" on page 19).

GESTURE
How to Bless Yourself

Recalling your Baptism in Christ, dip the forefingers of your right hand into the font, touching the water, and then bring it to your forehead, saying inaudibly, "In the name of the Father," then, tracing downward, touch your chest, "and of the Son," then, tracing toward the left shoulder, "and of the Holy," then, tracing toward the right shoulder, "Spirit. Amen."

What does it mean?

Amen is a Hebrew word that is used throughout the Mass and in Christian prayer that means "So be it."

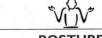

POSTURE
Genuflect or Bow

Genuflecting was an ancient sign of reverence toward an earthly ruler. The Church adopted it as a way of showing the ultimate reverence toward the true King — Our Lord. It is done by lowering ourselves and touching the right knee to the floor.

Bowing is another sign of reverence and is done by bending forward at the waist.

Opening Hymn

At the Mass, we die to ourselves to become one with all who are gathered as the one Body of Christ. Join in the singing of the opening hymn so that your voice becomes one with the rest. St. Paul wrote to the Colossians, "Let the word of Christ dwell in you richly, as you teach and admonish one another in all wisdom, and as you sing psalms and hymns and spiritual songs with thankfulness in your hearts to God" (Colossians 3:16).

POSTURE
Stand

We stand as a sign of respect (when an important person enters a room, we rise). Here, as the priest, representing Christ, enters, we stand.

But we will remain standing because standing was the normal posture of prayer for the Jewish people and the first followers of Christ (who were Jewish) continued this practice.

> *Standing is the other side of reverence toward God.*
> — *Sacred Signs,* Romano Guardini

The Sign of the Cross

Catholic prayer begins by recalling the saving act of Our Lord Jesus Christ on the cross. We make the Sign of the Cross with the priest.

SPEAKING THE BIBLE:

"Go therefore and make disciples of all nations, baptizing them in the name of the Father and of the Son and of the Holy Spirit, teaching them to observe all that I have commanded you; and

behold, I am with you always, to the close of the age" (Matthew 28:19–20).

Knowing this helps us to appreciate that when we make the Sign of the Cross and say this prayer we call to mind our Baptism, our duties as a follower of Christ, and the assurance of His presence throughout our lives.

We make the sign of the cross before we pray to collect and compose ourselves and to fix our minds and hearts and wills upon God. We make it when we finish praying in order that we may hold fast the gift we have received from God. In temptations we sign ourselves to be strengthened; in dangers, to be protected. The cross is signed upon us in blessings in order that the fullness of God's life may flow into the soul and fructify and sanctify us wholly.

— *Sacred Signs*, Romano Guardini

The Greeting

The priest greets us not with the words of our culture, like "Good morning" or "Good afternoon," but with the Word of God — that is, words taken from the Bible. This should make us aware of the sacred ritual we are entering into.

SPEAKING THE BIBLE:

"The grace of the Lord Jesus Christ and the love of God and the fellowship of the Holy Spirit be with you all" (2 Corinthians 13:14).

Or:

"The LORD be with you" (Ruth 2:4).

Our Response

Our response is taken from God's Word (the Bible). In the time of Jesus, it meant "and also with you," but early in the Church's history, "your spirit" came to be associated with the "spirit" conferred upon the ordained, and the response was only used to return their greeting.

SPEAKING THE BIBLE:

"The grace of our Lord Jesus Christ be **with your spirit**, brethren" (Galatians 6:18).

The Act of Penitence

We all are invited to make a general confession of our sinfulness before the Lord. There are different options the priest has in how this is done. They all conclude with the priest asking God to forgive our sins and to save us. No matter what form is used, the "Lord, Have Mercy" is a part of it.

SILENCE

A period of silent reflection occurs as we personally recollect how we have failed to trust in God's love for us.

GESTURE
Striking the Breast

If the first option of the act of penitence, The Confiteor, is used, we strike our breast when we declare it "through our fault." This is done simply by making a fist with the right hand and bringing it to your chest and striking it. In the Bible "striking one's breast" was a sign of mourning (see Luke 18:13; 23:48; and Zechariah 12:10). We mourn our failure to live up to God's grace.

> *The blow also is to wake us up. It is to shake the soul awake into the consciousness that God is calling, so that she may hear, and take his part and punish herself. She reflects, repents, and is contrite.*
> — *Sacred Signs*, Romano Guardini

SPEAKING THE BIBLE:

*"**Lord, have mercy** on my son, for he is an epileptic and he suffers terribly; for often he falls into the fire, and often into the water"* (Matthew 17:15).

*"The crowd rebuked them, telling them to be silent; but they cried out the more, '**Lord, have mercy** on us, Son of David!'"* (Matthew 20:31).

In both places where the "Lord, have mercy" occurs in the Bible, the people pleading with Jesus are in great need — as we speak this Word, we should be mindful of our total need for God.

The Gloria

This ancient hymn is sung or said unless it is during the Season of Advent or Lent. Here we have the song of the angels at Christmas, the declaration of John the Baptist, the cry of mercy from those sitting in darkness, the recalling of the resurrection of Christ and our share in it, the song of the Blessed in Heaven, and the declaration that God is God! This prayer is the whole story of salvation wrapped up in the praise of the Triune God.

SPEAKING THE BIBLE:

*"And suddenly there was with the angel a multitude of the heavenly host praising God and saying, **'Glory to God in the highest, and on earth peace among men with whom he is pleased!'"** (Luke 2:13–14).*

*"The next day he [John the Baptist] saw Jesus coming toward him, and said, 'Behold, **the Lamb of God**, who **takes away the sin of the world!'"** (John 1:29).*

*"And as Jesus passed on from there, two blind men followed him, crying aloud, **'Have mercy on us**, Son of David'"* (Matthew 9:27).

*"If then you have been raised with Christ, seek the things that are above, where Christ is, **seated at the right hand of God"** (Colossians 3:1).*

*"Who shall not fear and glorify your name, O Lord? **For you alone are holy**. All nations shall*

come to worship you, for your judgments have been revealed" (Revelation 15:4).

*"Let them know that **you alone**, whose name is the LORD, **are the Most High** over all the earth"* (Psalms 83:18).

The Collect
We are invited by the priest to pray with the words "Let us pray," and we pause in silence to do so.

SILENCE

We recollect ourselves joining our prayers to those of the priest.

What does it mean?
The Collect is the prayer that is often called the "Opening Prayer" in English. In it, the priest "collects" the prayers of the faithful and offers a prayer to God in the name of all.

THE LITURGY OF THE WORD

POSTURE
Sit

Sitting is the posture of listening and reflecting on what we are hearing. From the First Reading through the Second Reading, we remain seated in a posture of attentiveness.

What does it mean?

We hear the Word of God proclaimed during the Liturgy of the Word. In other words the Holy Bible is read to us:

- The First Reading is taken from the Old Testament or the Acts of the Apostles.
- The Responsorial Psalm is taken from the Book of Psalms.
- The Second Reading is taken from one of the New Testament Letters or the Book of Revelation.

- The Gospel is from one of the four Gospels.

After the First and Second Reading

There are many instances of the phrase, "The Word of the Lord," or "The Word of God," occurring in Scripture.

SPEAKING THE BIBLE:

*"And after some days Paul said to Barnabas, 'Come, let us return and visit the brethren in every city where we proclaimed **the word of the Lord**, and see how they are'"* (Acts 15:36).

Our Response to the First and Second Reading:

SPEAKING THE BIBLE:

*"**Thanks be to God** for his inexpressible gift!"* (2 Corinthians 9:15).

SILENCE

In the period of silence after the readings we meditate on the Scripture we have just heard.

Responsorial Psalm

What does it mean?

In between the First and Second Reading is the Responsorial Psalm, so called because, along with a psalm that is usually chanted by a cantor or choir, there is a response that is sung by the congregation. This psalm and our response are meant to help us further meditate on the readings we hear proclaimed.

The Acclamation before the Gospel

POSTURE
Stand

We rise to greet the Lord who is about to speak to us through His Gospel. Like those who greeted him with Alleluias on His glorious entrance into Jerusalem, we greet the procession of the Gospel book with our Alleluias.

> *When you are sitting down to rest or chat, and someone to whom you owe respect comes in and turns to speak to you, at once you stand up and remain standing so long as he is speaking and you are answering him.*
> — *Sacred Signs*, Romano Guardini

What does it mean?

Alleluia is the Greek form of the Hebrew *Hallelujah*, which means "Praise the Lord!" or, more literally, "Praise *Yahweh*!" *Yahweh* is the Hebrew sacred name for God.

Note: During the season of Lent, the Alleluia is not said but replaced with another acclamation that gives praise to God.

SPEAKING THE BIBLE:

"After this I heard what seemed to be the mighty voice of a great multitude in heaven, crying, 'Hal-lelujah! Salvation and glory and power belong to our God, for his judgments are true and just; he has judged the great harlot who corrupted the earth with her fornication, and he has avenged on her the blood of his servants'" (Revelation 19:1–2).

The Gospel

What does it mean?

Gospel is an Old English translation of the Greek *evangelion*, which means "good news."

SPEAKING THE BIBLE:

*"Then Philip opened his mouth, and beginning with this Scripture he told him **the good news** of Jesus"* (Acts 8:35).

Greeting of the Proclaimer of the Gospel

We are greeted by the deacon or priest who will proclaim the Gospel to us in the same way that we were greeted at the beginning of the Mass. He then announces where the Gospel of the day is taken from, and we respond by giving "glory" to the Lord.

SPEAKING THE BIBLE:

*"Let them **give glory to the LORD**, and declare his praise in the islands"* (Isaiah 42:12).

GESTURE
Signing our forehead, lips, and heart with the Sign of the Cross

We trace the sign of the cross on our forehead, lips, and heart as we say inaudibly, "May the Lord purify my understanding, my speech, and my heart, so that I may receive the words of the Gospel." This outward sign is meant to help us to focus on the words of Our Savior that we hear in the Gospel.

Our response to the Gospel
In response to the Gospel, we give praise to the Lord.

SPEAKING THE BIBLE:

*"And in the fourth year all their fruit shall be holy, an offering of **praise to the Lord**"* (Leviticus 19:24).

Homily

POSTURE
Sit

We reflect on the Gospel we have heard as the homilist "opens the Scriptures" to us.

What does it mean?

The English word homily comes from the Greek *homilia*, which simply means "discourse" — but in the Christian context, it came to mean a commentary on the Scriptures with the goal of explaining both the literal meaning of the texts and bringing out the spiritual meaning of them for us today.

The Nicene Creed

POSTURE
Stand

Nourished by the Word of God, we arise as we once did from the Baptismal font (if we were baptized as adults) to affirm our faith and trust in God and all that God has revealed.

What does it mean?

A creed is a set of beliefs; the Latin word *credo* means "I believe." Nicaea was the site of a universal council of the early Church in 325, and this creed is a product of that council as well as that of a later one held in Constantinople in 381.

SPEAKING THE BIBLE:

A few verses of the Creed are taken directly from the Scriptures:

*"Yet for us there is **one God**, the Father, from whom are all things and for whom we exist, and **one Lord, Jesus Christ**, through whom are all things and through whom we exist"* (1 Corinthians 8:6).

*"For in him **all things** were created, in **heaven and on earth, visible and invisible**"* (Colossians 1:16).

*"And in the synagogues immediately he proclaimed Jesus, saying, 'He is the **Son of God**'"* (Acts 9:20).

*"I am the bread which **came down from heaven**"* (John 6:41).

GESTURE
Bow

When we pray the Creed, we make a profound bow (bending at the waist) at the words "by the power of the Holy Spirit, he was born of the Virgin Mary, and became man," showing our respect for God becoming one of us (called the Incarnation). On the feasts of the Annunciation and the Nativity of the Lord (Christmas), we genuflect during these words as a special way of celebrating the mystery that these feasts commemorate.

Prayers of the Faithful

In the prayers of the faithful, we pray for the universal needs of the Church first and then the needs of the local church.

SPEAKING THE BIBLE:

*"**Lord, hear** my voice! Let your ears be attentive to the voice of my supplications!" (Psalms 130:2).*

THE LITURGY OF THE EUCHARIST

POSTURE
Sit

Unlike the posture we take to hear the Word of God and the homily, here we take the posture to give and to reflect on the question, "What is the Lord asking of me?"

The Preparation of the Gifts

The altar is prepared with a corporal, purificator, chalice, and missal. At the same time, a collection is taken among the congregation, and the gifts of bread and wine are prepared to be brought forth.

What is it?

- Corporal: A small, square, linen cloth that serves as a sacred place mat

- Purificator: A linen cloth used only for the cleaning of sacred vessels
- Chalice: A sacred cup used to hold the wine that will become the Blood of Christ
- Missal: A book that contains all the prayers used at Mass

The Collection

GESTURE
Giving

What we drop in the collection basket is a symbol of ourselves. Ultimately, it is our very life that we are to offer to God at this and every Mass.

SPEAKING THE BIBLE:

We may think that taking up the collection is not "speaking the Bible," but St. Paul in his Second Letter to the Corinthians, in chapters 8 and 9, has much to say about taking up a collection and sums it up with:

"Each one must do as he has made up his mind, not reluctantly or under compulsion, for God loves a cheerful giver" (2 Corinthians 9:7).

Offertory Procession

Representatives of the congregation bring up the gifts, and they are received by the priest. These gifts include:

- The bread that will be offered at this Mass
- The wine that will be offered at this Mass
- The gifts that we have offered for the support of the parish and the poor

The Preparation of the Gifts

The prayers that the priest says over the gifts may be said inaudibly. They are a Christian adaptation of ancient Jewish prayers used during the Sabbath celebration (and most likely used by Jesus Himself). If they are audible, we respond, "Blessed be God forever."

SPEAKING THE BIBLE:

*"Christ, who is **God** over all, **blessed for ever**"* (Romans 9:5).

POSTURE
Stand

We rise to join in the prayer over the gifts, asking God to accept the offering of the priest — which is not only his, but ours as well.

The Eucharistic Prayer

The *General Instruction of the Roman Missal*, the guide to the proper celebration of the Mass, calls the Eucharistic Prayer "the center and summit of the entire celebration"[4] of the Mass. In it, the priest:

- "Invites the people to lift up their hearts to the Lord in prayer and thanksgiving"[5]
- "Unites the congregation with himself in the prayer that he addresses in the name of the entire community to God the Father through Jesus Christ in the Holy Spirit"[6]

In this great prayer, we join ourselves with Jesus both in offering ourselves with Him in sacrifice and in proclaiming the trustworthiness of God by recounting all that He has done in the past.

The Preface

Most of the elements of this ancient part of the Eucharistic prayer, including the first part of the "Holy, Holy, Holy" date back to the time of Jesus, when parts of it were recited every morning in the Synagogue. The prayer is both an invitation to us to enter fully into the prayer and one of communal thanksgiving to God for all that God has done for us.

Sanctus

In response to all that the priest recounts God has done for us in the Preface, we now respond with a prayer that joins God's praise both in Heaven (see Isaiah 6:3 and Revelation 4:8 on page 51) and on Earth (see Matthew 21:9 on page 51).

What does it mean?

Sanctus is a Latin word that means "holy." *Hosanna* is a Hebrew word that means "Save us."

SPEAKING THE BIBLE:

"Holy, holy, holy is the Lord of hosts; the whole earth is full of his glory" (Isaiah 6:3).

"And the four living creatures, each of them with six wings, are full of eyes all round and within, and day and night they never cease to sing, 'Holy, holy, holy, is the Lord God Almighty, who was and is and is to come!'" (Revelation 4:8).

"And the crowds that went before him and that followed him shouted, 'Hosanna to the Son of David! Blessed is he who comes in the name of the Lord! Hosanna in the highest!'" (Matthew 21:9).

POSTURE
Kneel

We kneel at the conclusion of the *Sanctus* as a sign of reverence and adoration of the one true God.

The Hebrews regarded the knees as a symbol of strength. To bend the knee is, therefore, to bend our strength before the living God, an acknowledgment of the fact that all that we are we receive from Him. In important passages of the Old Testament, this gesture appears as an expression of worship.

— *The Spirit of the Liturgy*, Joseph Ratzinger (Pope Benedict XVI)

Epiclesis

During the Eucharistic Prayer, the priest prays to God that the Holy Spirit will come upon the gifts being offered so that they may become the Body and Blood of our Lord. As he prays this prayer, he places his hands palms down over the bread and wine and, as he concludes the prayer, makes the Sign of the Cross over them.

What does it mean?

Epiclesis is a Greek word that means to "invoke upon." In this part of the Eucharistic Prayer, the Holy Spirit is invoked upon the gifts being offered.

The Institutional Narrative and Consecration

What Christ instituted at the Last Supper is carried out by the Church in repeating His words and actions. As the priest recites the words of Jesus, we are present at the Sacrifice of Jesus on the cross at Calvary. The consecration of the bread and wine into the Body and Blood of Christ happens through the power of the words of Jesus and the action of the Holy Spirit. Though the outward signs of the bread and wine remain, we believe that the whole substance of both has been changed into the Body and Blood of Christ — the Church calls this mystery *transubstantiation*.

SPEAKING THE BIBLE:

*"Jesus took bread, and **blessed**, and **broke** it, and **gave** it to the **disciples** and said, 'Take, eat; this is my body.' And he took a **chalice**, and when he had given **thanks** he gave it to them, saying, 'Drink of it, all of you; for this is my blood of the covenant, which is poured out for many for the forgiveness of sins'"* (Matthew 26:26–28).

*"And as they were eating, he took **bread**, and **blessed**, and **broke** it, and **gave** it to them, and said, 'Take; this is my body.' And he **took** a **chalice**, and when he had **given thanks** he **gave** it to them, and they all drank of it. And he said to them, '**This is my blood of the covenant, which is poured out for many**'"* (Mark 14:22–24).

*"For I received from the Lord what I also delivered to you, that the Lord Jesus on the night when he was betrayed **took bread**, and when he had **given thanks**, he **broke** it, and said, '**This is my body which is for you. Do this in remembrance of me**.' In the same way also the chalice, after supper, **saying, 'This chalice is the new covenant in my blood. Do this, as often as you drink it, in remembrance of me**.' For as often as you eat this bread and drink the chalice, you proclaim the Lord's death until he comes"* (1 Corinthians 11:23–26).

You may perhaps say: "My bread is ordinary." But that bread is bread before the words of the Sacraments; where the consecration has entered in, the bread becomes the Flesh of Christ.

— *The Sacraments*, St. Ambrose

Anamnesis

The Eucharistic Prayer recalls God's saving work throughout history that culminates in the Passion and Resurrection of Jesus and awaits His return in glory. This "recalling" makes present this great mystery and our need to offer God thanksgiving and praise for all He has done and continues to do for us.

What does it mean?

Anamnesis is a Greek word that means "to remember."

Offering

In the Eucharistic Prayer, the Church offers to the Father, through the Holy Spirit, not only the "spotless Victim," Our Lord Jesus Christ, but also we who have been baptized in Christ — through this Mass, we die to ourselves so that we might live in Him. As the priest offers this part of the Eucharistic Prayer, make a conscious effort to offer yourself to God.

Intercessions

The needs of the entire Church are expressed to God in the Eucharistic Prayer. It is in this part of the prayer that you will hear the Pope being prayed for, as well as the bishop of the diocese, and all of the faithful — both the living and the dead.

The Great Amen

The Eucharistic Prayer ends with great praise given to God the Father, often sung, and the response of the faithful is an "Amen," called "great" because it is our assent to this great prayer that has brought Christ into our midst.

Amen is the people's signature.
— St. Augustine

The Communion Rite

POSTURE
Stand

We rise as the risen Lord rose from the dead. We stand to pray the prayer that He taught His disciples to pray.

On the first day of the week, we stand when we pray. The reason is that on the day of Resurrection, by standing at prayer, we remind ourselves of the grace we have received.
— St. Basil the Great

The Lord's Prayer

The priest invites us to pray in the words that Jesus taught His disciples (us) to pray.

SPEAKING THE BIBLE:

*"Pray then like this: **Our Father who art in heaven, Hallowed be thy name. Thy kingdom come. Thy will be done, On earth as it is in heaven. Give us this day our daily bread; And forgive us our trespasses, As we forgive those who trespass against us; And lead us not into temptation, But deliver us from evil"** (Matthew 6:9–15).

The priest continues to pray that we all might be delivered from every evil and blessed with the Lord's peace. To this prayer, we join a doxology that dates back to the early Church.

What does it mean?

Doxology is a Greek word that means "a word of praise."

SPEAKING THE BIBLE:

Some ancient texts (but not all) add the following, in some form, to Matthew's version of the Lord's Prayer:

"For thine is the kingdom and the power and the glory, for ever. Amen."

The Rite of Peace

The priest asks Jesus to look down upon us gathered and to grant us both the peace and the unity of God's Kingdom. He then offers us the peace of Christ, and the deacon or priest invites us to share the peace of Christ with those around us.

SPEAKING THE BIBLE:

*"Peace I leave with you; my peace I give to you;
not as the world gives do I give to you. Let not
your hearts be troubled, neither let them be
afraid"* (John 14:27).

GESTURE
Handshake

The sign of peace in the United States is
a handshake. Worshipers should greet those
around them, mindful of the symbolism of
the act — namely, that we are in communion
with one another and sharing the love that
Christ has given to us.

> *The spiritual embrace that all the worshippers give one another during the liturgy symbolizes in anticipation agreement, unity in faith, and love. It prefigures future blessings beyond words.*
> — St. Maximus the Confessor

The Fraction

The priest then takes the Body of Christ (under the outward appearance of bread) and breaks it into smaller pieces. This replicates the action of Jesus at the Last Supper and symbolizes that by partaking in this Eucharist, we become one with the Body of Christ — sharing in the one Bread broken.

The priest then breaks a small piece and places it into the chalice containing the Precious Blood of the Lord symbolizing the unity of the living Body of Christ. While he performs these actions, we say or sing the *Agnus Dei,* the "Lamb of God."

SPEAKING THE BIBLE:

*"The next day he saw Jesus coming toward him, and said, 'Behold, the **Lamb of God, who takes away the sin of the world!**'"* (John 1:29).

*"Have mercy upon us, O **LORD**, have **mercy** upon us, for we have had more than enough of contempt"* (Psalms 123:3).

*"**Grant us peace**"* (1 Maccabees 11:50).

GESTURE
Kneel

In most places, you will kneel at the conclusion of the Lamb of God (watch to see what the local custom is).[7]

Communion

SPEAKING THE BIBLE:

*"And the angel said to me, 'Write this: **Blessed are** those who are **invited** to the marriage **supper** of the Lamb'"* (Revelation 19:9).

*"Jesus went with them. When he was not far from the house, the centurion sent friends to him, saying to him, '**Lord**, do not trouble yourself, for **I am not worthy to have you come under my roof;** therefore I did not presume to come to you. **But say the word, and let my** servant **be healed.** For I am a man set under authority, with soldiers under me: and I say to one, "Go," and he goes; and to another, "Come," and he comes; and to my slave, "Do this," and he does it'"* (Luke 7:6–8).

GESTURE
Walking

We leave our seat to approach the priest, deacon, or extraordinary minister of the Eucharist to receive Our Lord in Holy Communion.

GESTURE
Bowing

Before receiving the Blessed Sacrament, we bow toward the Sacrament as a sign of reverence; if we receive from the cup, we repeat this gesture toward the Precious Blood before receiving it also.

GESTURE
Receiving Holy Communion

We respond to the words "The Body of Christ" or "The Blood of Christ" with "Amen." This is a sign of our agreement with all that the Church teaches and believes about Christ. We should not receive if we are conscious of any serious unconfessed sin or if we are not yet in full communion with the Catholic Church (in either of these instances, seek out a priest for help). We receive either by accepting the Blessed Sacrament in our hand and then immediately communicating or by having the priest place the Eucharist on our tongue. We similarly accept the cup, if we receive the Precious Blood, taking a small sip and then returning the cup to the minister. We then return to our seat and take up the accepted posture of the congregation.

SPEAKING THE BIBLE:

*"The bread which we break, is it not a participation in **the body of Christ**?"* (1 Corinthians 10:16).

*"The cup of blessing which we bless, is it not a participation in **the blood of Christ**?"* (1 Corinthians 10:16).

The congregation may observe a time of silent prayer or a time of communal thanksgiving (by singing a song of praise) once the distribution of Holy Communion is finished. Join in.

Prayer after Communion

We are invited by the priest to pray with the words, "Let us pray," and we pause in silence to do so.

POSTURE
Stand

We rise to show our unity.

SILENCE

Mindful of all that we have received at this Mass, we prepare to join our thanksgiving to that of the priest who prays in our name. We respond to this prayer with an "Amen."

CONCLUDING RITES

Once the priest has concluded the "Prayer after Communion," there may be announcements; if not, the priest will again greet us, and we respond as we have done throughout the Mass. He then blesses us, and we receive his blessing by responding with an "Amen." Then, a deacon or the priest announces that the Mass is ended, and we give thanks to God for sending us forth to share Christ with all whom we come into contact with in our lives.

SPEAKING THE BIBLE:

"Go therefore and make disciples of all nations, baptizing them in the name of the Father and of the Son and of the Holy Spirit" (Matthew 28:19).

"Thanks be to God through Jesus Christ our Lord!" (Romans 7:25).

A Prayer to Say after Mass

Lord, Father, all-powerful and ever-living God, I thank you, for even though I am a sinner, your unprofitable servant, not because of my worth but in the kindness of your mercy, you have fed me with the precious Body and Blood of your Son, our Lord Jesus Christ.

I pray that this communion may not bring me condemnation and punishment, but for-giveness and salvation. May it be a helmet of faith and a shield of good will. May it purify me from evil ways and put an end to my evil passions. May it bring me charity and patience, humility and obedience, and growth in the power to do good. May it be my strong defense against all my enemies, visible and invisible, and the perfect calming of all my evil impulses, bodily and spiritual. May it unite me more closely to you, the one true God, and lead me safely through death to everlasting happiness with you.

And I pray that you will lead me, a sinner, to the banquet where You, with Your Son and Holy Spirit, are true and perfect light, total fulfillment, everlasting joy, gladness without end, and perfect happiness to your saints. Grant this through Christ our Lord.

Amen.

— St. Thomas Aquinas

THE EMMAUS STORY: ENCOUNTERING THE RISEN CHRIST AT MASS

In his encyclical *On the Eucharist in Its Relationship to the Church*, Pope John Paul II said that "whenever the Church celebrates the Eucharist, the faithful can in some way relive the experience of the two disciples on the road to Emmaus: 'Their eyes were opened and they recognized (Jesus).'"[8] In Chapter 24 of Luke's Gospel is the account of two disciples traveling on the road to Emmaus on that first Easter Sunday.

What Was Their Experience?

Cleophas[9] and an unnamed disciple (tradition gives his name as Symeon) are traveling to a town named Emmaus some seven miles from Jerusalem. As the two men journey, they are joined by a stranger whom they do not recognize (we are told by Luke that it is Jesus).[10]

Isn't it strange that Jesus isn't recognized in many of the accounts of those who witnessed Him after the Resurrection? Mary Magdalene mistakes Him for a gardener;[11] the disciples don't recognize Him from the boat when He is on the seashore;[12] and here in the Gospel of Luke, we are told that that Cleophas and Symeon "were kept from recognizing Him." Our Lord had prophesied[13] that when he returns to judge the nations, those who are judged — both the good and the evil — will all cry in unison, "When did we see *you*, Lord?"[14]

The Bible presents the world in a very different way than we are apt to think of it. There is a sense of uncertainty that dominates the biblical world — one is never sure of the true identity of a person until later, as we shall see in the case of Joseph and Symeon here.

"This stranger" asks them what it is that they are discussing as they travel. "Looking sad," they tell him — and in doing so, they

pour out their hopes and grief, as well as their political and theological opinions on the matter. The stranger then takes them to task: *"O foolish men, and slow of heart to believe all that the prophets have spoken! Was it not necessary that the Christ should suffer these things and enter into his glory?"*[15]

The stranger has their attention. So they listen, wondering what He'll say next. He opens the Scriptures to them — He incarnates the Word, brings it down to their level. Later they'll reflect back to this moment when He opened the Scriptures to them and how their hearts burned within them.

They reach their destination, and it seems that the stranger is going to go further. Our Lord is always going further than we want to go! And then comes one of the more scandalous points in this often-told story. The *Second Catholic Edition of the Revised Standard Version of the Bible* translates the Greek passage, "But they constrained him,"[16] which captures something of what they do, because the Greek word that is translated "constrained" connotes violence of force. There are a number of ways to think of this. Think of the violent onslaught of a crowd of fans to get near a superstar — this could be what Luke intends. But I think it is more than that. I think it is a clear sign that Cleophas and Symeon learned well the lesson of the stranger's homily on the Passion of the Lord — and now they forcibly "arrest" the stranger forcing Him to stay with them. The way the Lord had been treated was a scandal to them at the start of the journey. But once the Scriptures were opened to them, they learned that it was God's will that Jesus be handed over and so treated. Our Lord willed to put Himself into the hands of humans both on Good Friday and again on Easter Sunday!

Now, at the table, the stranger (whom they still do not recognize) takes bread, gives thanks, breaks it, and gives it to them.

They recognize Him. It is the Lord! Then He disappears from their midst physically, but the Bread remains: "This is my Body!"

They run back to Jerusalem to tell the apostles what they have heard and seen, and how He was made known to them in the "breaking of the bread."[17]

How We Can Relive This Experience at Every Mass

Did you realize that this story of the Risen Christ found in Luke's Gospel follows the structure of the Mass?[18] In fact, it gives us an excellent guide for encountering Our Lord at every Mass:

- The disciples gather like we do when we come to Mass.
- They bring their cares and concerns with them.
- The Lord opens the Scriptures to them (the Liturgy of the Word).
- They invite the Lord to stay with them (the Offertory).
- He takes the bread and gives thanks (the Eucharistic Prayer).
- The bread is broken (the Lamb of God).
- They recognize His presence, as we do at Holy Communion.

- They go forth to spread the good news, as we do when we are sent forth.

Like the disciples on their journey to Emmaus, we all enter the Church on any given day with our own ideas about who Jesus is and what Jesus should be doing in our lives and the lives of those around us. We probably wouldn't recognize Christ if he was in our midst because of all of our preconceived notions. We need to hear Him when he says, "O foolish men." We have much to confess, and we ask the Lord's mercy when we come together in His midst — "where two or three are gathered" in His name — and He is there.

Letting go of "what we think" is important as we hear the Word of God proclaimed at Mass and have the Scriptures opened to us. The dying to self that Jesus demanded can only take place at Mass when we realize that the Act of Penitence with which we begin every Mass is no empty ritual, but a necessary door to truly experiencing His presence in the Word and the Sacrament.

We open ourselves to what He reveals about Himself, and then we beg Him to stay with us. We receive Him in the Breaking of the Bread, and we realize that we will encounter Him again as we go forth to evangelize.

Once we realize *"Whom"* the Mass is all about, we will find that our hearts burn within us as His Sacred Heart sets our hearts on fire.

Notes

[1] Joseph Ratzinger, *The Spirit of the Liturgy* (San Francisco: Ignatius Press, 2000), p. 23.

[2] Ibid., p. 23.

[3] *Sacrosanctum concilium*, 47.

[4] *General Instruction of the Roman Missal*, 78.

[5] *General Instruction of the Roman Missal*, 78.

[6] *General Instruction of the Roman Missal*, 78.

[7] *General Instruction of the Roman Missal*, 43. In dioceses of the United States, the bishop of a diocese may mandate another posture. If you are traveling, look to see what everyone else is doing at this time.

[8] *Ecclesia De Eucharistia*, 6.

[9] Eusebius tells us that Cleophas was the brother of St. Joseph, the foster father of Jesus, and that Symeon was his son. Symeon also was the successor of St. James as bishop of Jerusalem. Both men died martyrs.

[10] Luke 24:15–16.

[11] John 20:15.

[12] John 21:4.

[13] Matthew 25:31–45.

[14] For an excellent book of meditations based on Matthew 25, read Bishop Robert J. Baker and Father Benedict J. Groeschel, C.F.R., *When Did We See You, Lord?* (Huntington, IN: Our Sunday Visitor, 2005).

[15] Luke 24:25–26.

[16] Luke 24:29.

[17] Luke 24:35.

[18] I use this in my book, *The How-To Book of the Mass* (Huntington, IN: Our Sunday Visitor, 2002, 2007), giving a running meditation on the Mass.